RUBANK EDUCATIONAL
LIBRARY No. 296

ONLINE MEDIA INCLUDED
Audio Recordings
Printable Piano Accompaniments

Concert and Contest COLLECTION

T0080118

for

TROMBONE
with piano accompaniment

Compiled and Edited

by **H. VOXMAN**

PLAYBACK+
Speed · Pitch · Balance · Loop

To access recordings and PDF accompaniments visit:
www.halleonard.com/mylibrary

3772-2638-5534-5837

ISBN 978-1-4234-7724-2

7777 W. BLUEMOUND RD. P.O. BOX 13819 MILWAUKEE, WI 53213

Visit Hal Leonard Online at
www.halleonard.com

COLLECTIONS IN THIS SERIES:

C Flute and Piano

B♭ Clarinet and Piano

B♭ Bass Clarinet and Piano

Oboe and Piano

Bassoon and Piano

E♭ Alto Saxophone and Piano

B♭ Tenor Saxophone and Piano

B♭ Cornet, Trumpet
or Baritone and Piano
(Baritone In Bass or Treble Clef)

French Horn (In F) and Piano

Trombone (Bass Clef) and Piano

E♭ or BB♭ Bass
(Tuba - Sousaphone) and Piano

Viola and Piano

Individually Compiled and Edited, Each Of the Collections Includes A Diversified Repertoire
The Solo Parts and Piano Accompaniments Are Published As Separate Books With A Durable Cover

Après un Rêve
(After A Dream)

Trombone

GABRIEL FAURÉ, Op. 7, No. 1
Transcribed by H. Voxman

Valse Sentimentale

Trombone

P. I. TSCHAIKOWSKY
Transcribed by H. Voxman

Canzonetta

Trombone

W. A. MOZART
Adapted by H. Voxman

Two Spanish Dances

Trombone

LEROY OSTRANSKY

I

II

Allegro

Thème de Concours

Trombone

ROBERT CLÉRISSE
Edited by H. Voxman

Sarabande and Vivace

Trombone

G. F. HANDEL
Transcribed by H. Voxman

Love Thoughts

Trombone

ARTHUR PRYOR
Transcribed by Clair W. Johnson

Morceau de Concours

Trombone

EDMOND MISSA
Edited by H. Voxman

*Eb in + 6th position,
lip trill to F.

Crépuscule
(Twilight)

Trombone

GABRIEL PARÈS
Edited by H. Voxman

Concerto Miniature

Trombone

LEROY OSTRANSKY

Prelude and Fanfaronade

Trombone

PAUL KOEPKE

Solo de Concert

Trombone

Th. DUBOIS
Edited by H. Voxman

Concerto in F Minor

Trombone

ÉMILE LAUGA
Edited by H. Voxman

Allegro Vivace
from Concerto

Trombone

Edited by H. Voxman

N. RIMSKY-KORSAKOFF
Arr. by N. Fedossejew